THIS IS NOT A LOVE STORY

Compilation and edits by
MARIANA GÓMEZ

To order additional copies of this book, contact:
Xlibris
1-888-795-4274
www.Xlibris.com
Orders@Xlibris.com

A special thank you to all the photographers and models for letting me share their awesome talent.

Another thank you to Professor Shelley for her guidance.

One more thank you to my parents and my friends for supporting my craziness.

Finally, the last thank you to Sarah Bahbah (IG @sarahbahbah) for inspiring me with her incredible artwork and techniques.

Dear, reader.

This book does not only tell one story, but it tells as many as one allows it to.

It could tell a story if read from beginning to end, or tell many others if paying individual attention to every page.

Let your imagination fly and enjoy.

Photography: Umar Sayyad
Model(s): Mariana Gómez and Noe Noe Aung
Location: Golden Drops Café

Photography: Umar Sayyad
Model(s): Mariana Gómez
Location: Golden Drops Café

Photography: Frida Ramírez
Model(s): Mariana Gómez and Alejandro García

Photography: Verónica Ruíz
Model(s): Mariana Gómez and Alejandro García

-You see how she bullies me?
[she jumps into his arms while laughing]
-Shut up. I still hate blue eyes.

Photography: Verónica Ruíz
Model(s): Mariana Gómez and Alejandro García

[indistinct Italian singing in the back]

Photography: Verónica Ruíz
Model(s): Mariana Gómez and Alejandro García

[Latin music plays]
-Dance with me.

Photography: Frida Ramírez
Model(s): Mariana Gómez and Alejandro García

[gets self-conscious about red lipstick and conservative society]

Photography: Frida Ramírez
Model(s): Mariana Gómez and Alejandro García

NARRATOR
It's funny 'cause then, it hit me.

Photography: Verónica Ruíz
Model(s): Mariana Gómez

Photography: Mariana Gómez
Model(s): Mariana Gómez

NARRATOR

He was in the art I hadn't made.

Photography: Tyler Judson
Model(s): Mariana Gómez
Art: Rae Malone

[dramatically watches the sunset]

Photography: Renata Gómez
Model(s): Mariana Gómez

Photography: Aadarsh Santosh
Model(s): Mariana Gómez, Shalaka Nallakandy Churai and Noe Noe Aung

-Me hangover? Please, I'm fresh as lettuce.
[carousel music playing]

Photography: Paulina Pedraza-Lecanda
Model(s): Mariana Gómez

Photography: Aadarsh Santosh
Model(s): Leandro Tapia and Noe Noe Aung

Photography: Aadarsh Santosh
Model(s): Shalaka Nallakandy Churai and Rae Malone

Photography: Paulina Pedraza-Lecanda
Model(s): Mariana Gómez and Natalia Reneaum

Photography: Paulina Pedraza-Lecanda
Model(s): Mariana Gómez and Natalia Reneaum

[does 2987 mistakes]

Photography: Vazia Grissom
Model(s): Mariana Gómez

Photography: Renata Gómez
Model(s): Mariana Gómez

[with a bad British accent]
-Nonsense, darling. Of course I'll marry you.

Photography: FamyaDivine
Model(s): Mariana Gómez

Photography: FamyaDivine
Model(s): Mariana Gómez

[screams underwater]

Photography: Renata Gómez
Model(s): Mariana Gómez

[gets lost in inner thoughts]

Photography: Renata Gómez
Model(s): Mariana Gómez

NARRATOR:
Reality was spinning.

Photography: Daniel Aristizabal
Model(s): Mariana Gómez
Art: Mariah A. Lynch

[about to turn twenty]
-Holly s**t, I'm old.

Photography: Daniel Aristizabal
Model(s): Mariana Gómez
Art: Mariah A. Lynch

[paints nails and misses]
[curses in Spanish]

Photography: Mariana Gómez
Model(s): Mariana Gómez

[can't get both eyes symmetrical]

Photography: Tyler Judson
Model(s): Mariana Gómez

-He loves me, he loves me not?

Photography: Umar Sayyad
Model(s): Mariana Gómez and Noe Noe Aung
Location: Golden Drops Café

-F**k that.
[slurps and coughs]

Photography: Umar Sayyad
Model(s): Mariana Gómez and Noe Noe Aung
Location: Golden Drops Café

[starts a chain of endless bad jokes]

Photography: Mariana Gómez
Model(s): Noe Noe Aung and Leandro Tapia

-This weekend easily beats any reality show.

Photography: Aadarsh Santosh
Model(s): Noe Noe Aung and Rae Malone

-Remember that time when we..
[interrupts with really loud laughter]
-I know exactly what you mean.

Photography: Paulina Pedraza-Lecanda
Model(s): Mariana Gómez and Natalia Reneaum

Photography: Paulina Pedraza-Lecanda
Model(s): Mariana Gómez and Natalia Reneaum
Location: McDonald's

-Man, I just adopted a bee.

Photography: Sabrina Fattal
Model(s): Mariana Gómez

[laugh for 5 minutes straight]
-Why are we like this?

Photography: Taji Harris
Model(s): Noe Noe Aung and Mariana Gómez

-And that's how I ...

Photography: Umar Sayyad
Model(s): Mariana Gómez and Noe Noe Aung
Location: Golden Drops Café

-Wait, what was the question?

Photography: Umar Sayyad
Model(s): Mariana Gómez and Noe Noe Aung
Location: Golden Drops Café

THE END.

... or beginning?

… wait, what?

… season two?…

and then what?…

f**k spoilers…

ugh, whatever…

TOLD
YOU

Printed in the United States
By Bookmasters